21st Century Skills **INNOVATION** *Library*

From Sharks to . . . Swimsuits

by Wil Mara

INNOVATIONS FROM   NATURE

Published in the United States of America by Cherry Lake Publishing
Ann Arbor, Michigan
www.cherrylakepublishing.com

Content Adviser: Robert Friedel, PhD, Professor of History, University of Maryland, College Park, Maryland

Design: The Design Lab

Photo Credits: Cover (main) and page 3, ©AP Photo/John D McHugh; cover (inset), ©Ian Scott/ Shutterstock, Inc.; page 4, ©Vlad Turchenko/Shutterstock, Inc.; page 6, ©YanLev/Shutterstock, Inc.; page 7, ©iStockphoto.com/microgenmicrogen; page 9, ©Schmid Christophe/Shutterstock, Inc.; page 10, ©A Cotton Photo/Shutterstock, Inc.; page 13, ©PRNewsFoto/SPEEDO; page 14, ©Chris Pole/Shutterstock, Inc.; page 16, ©AP Photo/Kathy Willens; pages 17 and 25, ©AP Photo/CTK, Rene Volfik; page 18, ©AP Photo/Mark J. Terrill; page 20, ©kbrowne41/Shutterstock, Inc.; page 21, ©luigi nifosi'/Shutterstock, Inc.; page 22, ©Jose Gil/Shutterstock.com; page 27, ©Georgios Kollidas/Shutterstock, Inc.; page 29, ©Mark William Penny/Shutterstock, Inc.

Library of Congress Cataloging-in-Publication Data
Mara, Wil.
 From sharks to . . . swimsuits/by Wil Mara.
    p. cm.–(Innovations from nature) (Innovation library)
 Includes bibliographical references and index.
 ISBN 978-1-61080-499-8 (lib. bdg.) – ISBN 978-1-61080-586-5 (e-book) –
ISBN 978-1-61080-673-2 (pbk.)
 1. Textile fabrics–Technological innovations–Juvenile literature. 2. Bathing suits–Design–Juvenile literature. 3. Scales (Fishes)–Juvenile literature. 4. Frictional resistance (Hydrodynamics)–Juvenile literature. I. Title.
 TS1767.M37 2012
 677'.02864–dc23   2012007365

Cherry Lake Publishing would like to acknowledge
the work of The Partnership for 21st Century Skills.
Please visit www.21stcenturyskills.org for more information.

Printed in the United States of America
Corporate Graphics Inc.
July 2012
CLFA11

CONTENTS

INNOVATIONS FROM NATURE

CHAPTER ONE

Yesterday and Today

Swimming is a fun and refreshing way to exercise.

Swimming is one of the healthiest and most enjoyable activities you can do. Millions of people around the world swim every day. You can swim in a pool, a lake, or a mighty ocean. You can race your friends, explore under the water's surface with a mask and snorkel, or just relax and float on your back. And what do you wear when you go swimming? A swimsuit, of course!

There are many different types of swimsuits. There are those for boys and girls, and those for adults. There are one-piece suits and two-piece suits. Some are just one color, and others are a dazzling variety of shades and patterns. Some are baggy, and others are so tight they look as though they've been painted on!

Swimsuits serve many purposes. In addition to when you are swimming, you can wear swimsuits when doing other water sports such as surfing, scuba diving, and waterskiing. A swimsuit provides cover for people trying to get a suntan and for those who want to show off their bodies in a beauty contest. And, of course, they are worn in swimming competitions.

Outfits designed specifically for swimming have been around for hundreds of years. In the 1600s, women in Europe wore suits made of canvas that covered nearly every inch of their body below the neck. In the 1860s in Great Britain, men wore shorts very similar to the swimsuits worn by men today.

In the early 1900s, an Australian swimmer named Annette Kellerman visited America. She wore a one-piece swimsuit that left her arms and legs exposed. This was considered pretty wild for the time, and poor Annette was even arrested for it! She launched a line of similar suits for women that became known as Kellermans. These were the earliest versions of the one-piece women's suit that is commonly worn today. Kellermans also began a "shrinking" trend in bathing suits, where every few years, suits gradually covered less and less of a person's body.

Even though bikinis have become common, many women still prefer one-piece swimsuits.

Divers wear swimsuits that will flex along with their bodies as they perform complicated twists and turns in the air.

During this time, some women wanted a swimsuit that was two pieces instead of one, leaving the midsection bare. This led to the creation of the bikini sometime in the late 1940s. Manufacturers also began experimenting with various fabrics in order to provide a better fit and greater comfort.

21st Century Content

 Designing clothes can be an interesting career choice. It involves working with a variety of beautiful fabrics while pushing your creative skills to their limits. You'll be challenged to design fashions that are not just pleasing to the eye, but also functional and comfortable. The best designers are expected to have a sense of what will be popular with the public in the future, as it often takes months or even years to get a new line of clothing into stores. Sometimes you will be required to travel to faraway places and study trends in other cultures. Some designers work alone, whereas others work as part of a team. Having an idea for a new shirt or pair of slacks one day, and then seeing it hanging in a store window on another, is one of the most rewarding experiences imaginable. And since consumers will always have an interest in "what's new," clothing designers will always be in demand!

Some swimsuits are designed specifically to aid swimmers during competitive water sports such as swimming and diving. These suits provide a very tight fit so that the body can move more easily and naturally. And while such suits offer very little in the way of bodily protection, they are made with material that creates as little **resistance** in the water as possible. When a swimmer enters the water, his or her body will meet with resistance, which will result in something called **drag**. Drag will slow down the swimmer and force him or her to use more energy in order to keep moving forward. Competitive swimwear should reduce drag as much as possible.

Amazingly, in the ongoing effort to improve upon existing swimwear technology, one person got help from one of the most fearsome creatures on Earth.

CHAPTER TWO

The Skinny on the Skin

In the late 1990s, 27-year-old Englishwoman Fiona Fairhurst was working for one of the world's leading swimsuit manufacturers. Fairhurst had studied **textiles** in college and was trying to find a way to make her company's swimsuits "faster." Any swimsuit, regardless of how advanced the technology, will produce some degree of drag and slow down the person wearing it. Fairhurst

Even the best swimsuits can slow down a swimmer.

A shark's skin helps it glide smoothly through the water.

wanted to find a way to reduce the drag as much as possible.

With the aid of scientific expertise in **hydrodynamics** provided by Jane Cappaert, a researcher at the International Center for Aquatic Research, Fairhurst got to work. She turned to a computer simulation known as CFD, or computational fluid dynamics. The simulator did a good job of predicting the behavior of certain materials used as swimwear in the water.

Fairhurst also decided to explore the world of plants and animals for answers. The practice of using nature as a model to create or improve upon human-made items is known as **biomimicry**. During her research, Fairhurst visited a natural history museum and studied the skin of sharks. She knew that sharks, one of nature's most efficient killers, were also superb swimmers. In the past, swimsuit manufacturers had produced suits with very smooth surfaces. What surprised her, then, was discovering that a shark's skin felt fairly rough.

Upon closer examination with a microscope, Fairhurst saw that sharkskin was made up of thousands upon thousands of tiny scales. Each scale had a set of **horizontal** (running side to side) ridges. These, she learned, were called **denticles**, and they played a key role in a shark's rapid movement. When water flows over

Learning & Innovation Skills

 Inventing a new product that people are willing to buy and use takes lots of hard work. Even when you get the first idea for something new, it can take many years to actually create a product that works. Thomas Edison, one of the greatest inventors in history, failed hundreds of times before he made a lightbulb that worked well. He did not consider those other bulbs to be failures, however, but rather a normal part of the creative process. Fiona Fairhurst was no different. She and her company experimented with more than 400 different types of fabrics, made nearly a dozen different swimsuits, and spent hundreds of thousands of dollars before they came up with the Fastskin. The moral of the story is that if you believe in your idea, be persistent and never give up!

a smooth surface, it breaks up into tiny swirls called **vortices**. These vortices contribute to drag. Fairhurst realized that the ridges on a shark's scales channel water more rapidly and efficiently. This reduces the rate of drag and enables sharks to swim at greater speed.

Using the CFD simulator, Fairhurst tested a swimsuit made from material that mimicked, or imitated, the denticled scales of sharkskin. Sure enough, the amount of drag in the simulation decreased, and the speed of the swimmer increased. Now all Fairhurst needed to do was construct a real suit to prove her theory. As she designed it, she also made sure it would fit tightly enough so that water would not get between the suit and the skin of the person wearing it.

Fairhurst eventually came up with the world's first "Fastskin" swimsuit. It was a huge success.

The suit was tested by some of the best swimmers in the world and found to reduce drag by nearly 5 percent. That might not sound like much, but in swimming competitions such as the Olympics, it could mean the difference between winning and losing a gold medal.

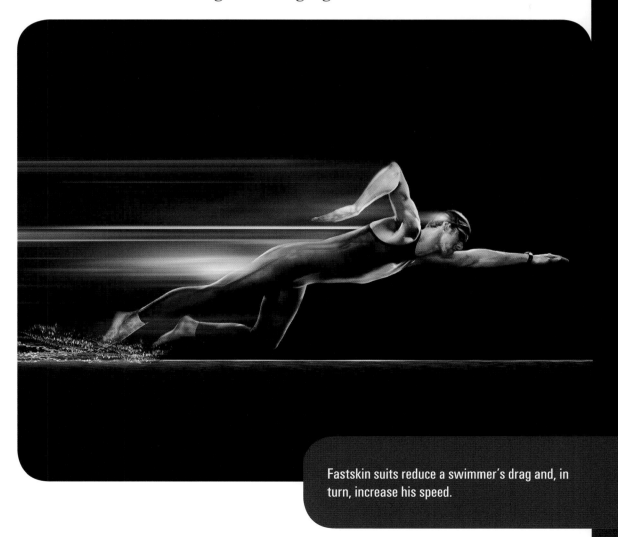

Fastskin suits reduce a swimmer's drag and, in turn, increase his speed.

CHAPTER THREE

Ups and Downs

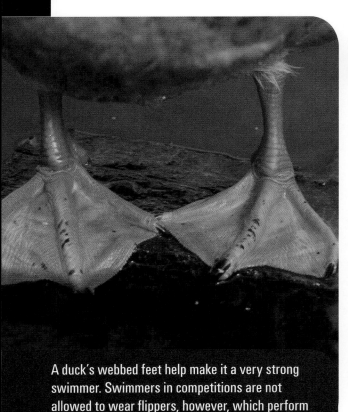

A duck's webbed feet help make it a very strong swimmer. Swimmers in competitions are not allowed to wear flippers, however, which perform the same function as webbing.

Fairhurst's Fastskin suit was an incredible development in the design of competitive swimwear. And yet, as hard as it may be to believe, not everybody was thrilled with it.

In the 2000 Olympic Summer Games, Fairhurst's company enthusiastically provided 150 athletes with the new swimsuit. They assured the swimmers that the shark-based fabric would give them an edge over their competitors. However, complaints began pouring in that anyone wearing the Fastskin suit would have an unfair advantage over other swimmers, which was a violation of Olympic rules. Specifically, there was a rule stating that swimmers were not allowed to use any "device" that aided them during competition. Such items included fins and flippers. It also included gloves with webbing between the fingers—another example of biomimicry, as many animals that swim well, such as frogs and ducks, have webbed feet.

Fairhurst's company argued that the Fastskin suit was not really a device but simply an improved type of swimming "costume." Many did not agree, however, and a case was eventually brought before a group of people known as the Court of Arbitration for Sport (CAS), which made final rulings concerning such matters. Meanwhile, swimmers hoping to compete in the Olympic Games were allowed to wear the Fastskin suit during tryouts. However, if the CAS decided that the Fastskins were against the rules, then the swimmers would have to either undergo another round of tryouts or be disqualified.

The prospects for the Fastskin suit looked grim. One college professor examined the suit carefully and felt that it did violate Olympic rules and therefore should be banned. In the end, however, the CAS decided that the

Fastskin was a legal form of swimwear and could be used. The fact that *any* swimmer could wear one if he or she chose probably had a bearing on their ruling.

Fiona Fairhurst and her revolutionary swimsuit have been publicly recognized and rewarded in many ways over the years. In *Popular Science* magazine, which has

Many professional swimmers now use Fastskin swimsuits.

Fiona Fairhurst was nominated for the 2009 European Inventor of the Year award for her incredible swimsuit.

Fastskin suits have helped such Olympic swimmers as Michael Phelps to achieve new records.

followed leading technological trends for more than a century, the suit earned a place on its *100 Best of What's New* list. Fairhurst also won the Pentland Group Product Excellence Award. Then, in 2009, she became a finalist (among thousands of candidates) for the title of European Inventor of the Year. She eventually left the company for whom she designed the Fastskin and started one of her own. It focuses on athletic wear for swimming as well as a wide variety of other sports.

Learning & Innovation Skills

 More than 80 percent of the swimming medals won at the 2000 Olympic Summer Games were won by swimmers wearing Fastskin. Some swimmers even set new world records! Four years later, at the Summer Olympics in Greece, an updated version of the suit—the Fastskin II—helped more than 40 athletes become medal winners and break even more records. It was clear that sharkskin technology signaled a new era in competitive swimming and possibly many other sports as well.

CHAPTER FOUR

Looking into the Future

Sharks will likely inspire other new and innovative technologies in the future.

Designers of competition swimwear are far from the only people interested in the potential of sharkskin-related technology. As with many other examples of biomimicry, human-made sharkskin is being considered in countless other industries.

Boat manufacturers believe that applying human-made sharkskin to

Like swimsuits, boats are affected by drag and may therefore also benefit from design ideas based on sharkskin.

the bottoms of their crafts may improve performance. Copying the ridged surface of a shark's scales should reduce drag so that a boat could reach greater speed while using less power. But there's another reason, too: the skin

Sharkskin-inspired designs might also help to improve fuel efficiency in automobiles.

of a shark has a natural tendency to fight off the buildup of foreign **organisms**. Tiny creatures in the sea often attach themselves to larger animals. These tiny organisms have a much harder time doing this on the body of a shark, though. One reason is because water flows over a shark's skin very rapidly. The unevenness of a shark's skin also makes it difficult for organisms to find a place where they can make contact. Additionally, the flexibility of a shark's skin and a shark's constant motion make it even more difficult for tiny critters to "get a grip."

Auto manufacturers have wondered about the benefits of using sharkskin on their products. If applied to the body of a car, perhaps such material would move air over it more efficiently, giving vehicles a bit more speed without burning as much fuel.

The medical industry is also interested in sharkskin material. By covering the surfaces of equipment as well

Learning & Innovation Skills

Perhaps the greatest challenge to the future of sharkskin technology involves sharks themselves. There are more than 300 shark species in the world, and millions of sharks are hunted and killed every year. An alarming number of these species are **endangered**—and are heading toward **extinction**. Scientists are convinced that sharks offer the key to unlocking many other secrets beyond the design of better swimwear. If these graceful and fascinating animals continue to be killed in such high numbers, however, we may lose the chance to unlock their secrets forever.

as certain environments (such as the walls and ceilings of an operating room), microorganisms that are potentially dangerous would have a much harder time establishing themselves. Such surfaces would also be ideal for public areas like schools and supermarkets. Another advantage is that less time, energy, and money could be spent cleaning these places. It's important to understand that sharkskin-type material only *fights off* harmful organisms. It doesn't kill them. This is actually beneficial. When organisms are killed, the survivors often adapt by becoming stronger, and then the problems they cause become much worse.

CHAPTER FIVE

The Best and the Brightest

Many people have made invaluable contributions to the worlds of athletic gear and biomimicry. Without these types of original thinkers, many of today's most innovative creations would not exist.

Fiona Fairhurst was born and raised in England, where she attended the University of Huddersfield, and Central St. Martins.

Fiona Fairhurst proved that original thinking is the key to innovation.

There she studied textile technology. Shortly after graduating, she was hired by one of the world's leading manufacturers of swimwear. An avid swimmer herself, her ability to "think outside the box" contributed to the development of sharkskin technology.

Leonardo da Vinci (1452–1519), the famous painter of the *Mona Lisa,* was also a sculptor, engineer, mathematician, musician, mapmaker, and inventor. Da Vinci kept notebooks that contained hundreds of his observations and sketches, and he strongly believed that many of humankind's problems could be solved through careful study of plants and animals. His sketches of machines that he believed could fly—early forerunners of today's modern aircraft—were based in part on his study of birds. Although he did not actually produce a working airplane, he clearly understood the basics of biomimicry and noted its value for future generations.

Janine Benyus (1958–) was born in New Jersey, and went on to become a professor at the University of Montana. She is one of the world's foremost experts on biomimicry, having written several books on the subject. She has also helped establish two organizations to further advance the study of biomimicry. The Biomimicry Guild is a company that aids in the development of products

Leonardo da Vinci is remembered as both a brilliant inventor and an amazing artist.

based on natural principles. The nonprofit Biomimicry Institute helps to promote biomimicry concepts, not just in business but among the public at large. Benyus

21st Century Content

 There is little doubt that technologies based on biomimicry are going to play a starring role in the future of humanity. Many of these technologies will be "green friendly," meaning they will do little or no harm to the environment while providing benefits to people everywhere. If you want to take part in these fascinating innovations and "ride the wave" of biomimicry, study the natural sciences. Then consider a career in fields where you can put your talents to good use. Such fields include engineering, environmental research, teaching, and a variety of medical professions.

has been honored with countless awards and featured in numerous newspaper and magazine articles. When she's not teaching or writing, she serves as a naturalist guide, works to protect public lands, and gives lectures at a variety of conferences and seminars.

What else do you think sharks can teach us?

Glossary

biomimicry (bye-oh-MI-mi-kree) the practice of copying nature in order to build or improve something

denticles (DEN-ti-kuhlz) tiny structures found on shark skin that are made of material similar to teeth

drag (DRAG) the force caused by water resistance on a moving object

endangered (en-DAYN-jerd) low in numbers with the threat of becoming lower

extinction (ek-STINGT-shun) no longer living or in use

horizontal (hor-uh-ZON-tuhl) flat and parallel to the ground

hydrodynamics (hye-dro-dye-NAM-iks) the study of liquids in motion and the forces acting on solid bodies in fluids

organisms (OR-guh-niz-uhmz) living plants or animals

resistance (ri-ZISS-tuhnss) a force that opposes the motion of an object

textiles (TEK-stilez) fabrics or cloths that have been woven or knitted

vortices (VOR-tih-seez) swirling masses of water or air

For More Information

BOOKS

Freese, Susan M. *Fashion*. San Francisco: Essential Library, 2009.

Lee, Dora. *Biomimicry: Inventions Inspired by Nature*. Tonawanda, NY: Kids Can Press, 2011.

Marsico, Katie. *Sharks*. New York: Children's Press, 2012.

Wagner, Kathi. *The Everything Kids' Shark Book: Dive into Fun-Infested Waters!* Avon, MA: Adams Media, 2005.

WEB SITES

Ask Nature—What Is Biomimicry?
www.asknature.org/article/view/what_is_biomimicry
Find out more about biomimicry, with examples, further links, and interesting video content.

Biomimicry Institute and Biomimicry Guild
www.biomimicry.net
Check out the latest news on the science of biomimicry, with links to other sites as well as information for those interested in choosing a career in the field.

Index

About the Author

Wil Mara is the award-winning author of more than 120 books, many of which are educational titles for young readers. More information about his work can be found at www.wilmara.com.